Hylas Publishing
First published in 2005 by Hylas Publishing®
129 Main St., Ste. C, Irvington NY 10533

Publisher: Sean Moore
Creative Director: Karen "Saltshaker" Prince
Art Director: Gus "Escobedo" Yoo
Designer: Joaquín Ramon Herrera
Editor: Gail Greiner
Proofreader: Angda Goel

First American Edition published in 2005.
02 03 04 05 10 9 8 7 6 5 4 3 2 1

Library of Congress Cataloging-in-Publication Data

Herrera, Joaquín Ramon
  Scary : a book of horrible things for kids / Joaquín
Ramon Herrera.—1st ed.
      p. cm.
 ISBN 1-59258-148-X
   Curiosities and wonders—Juvenile literature. I. Title.
 G243.H395 2005
 1.02—dc22

ISBN: 1-59258-148-X

d and Bound in the United States of America
uted in the United States by National Book Network.
uted in Canada by Kate Walker & Company, Ltd.

SCARY

A Book of Horrible Things For Kids

R

1
AC
03

ISB

All
Cop
repr
any
copy
proje
sion

Printe
Distri
Distrib

SCARY

A Book of Horrible Things For Kids

Written and Illustrated by
Joaquín Ramon Herrera

AND HORRIS

"Tell the children the truth."
– Robert Nesta Marley

for jeremiah joaquín,
rainsong eva,
and
ethan joaquín

beautiful souls born into a very scary world

TABLE OF CONTENTS

Places Where the Shadows Grow

The Things We've Done

Imagine This...If You Dare

JOAQUIN'S INTRODUCTION

Hello, my friend. Welcome. I am absolutely thrilled that you have chosen to join me on this little walk down a somewhat dark and unpredictable path. I think you are in for a very interesting and exciting time.

I must admit, most of what you will read about is just a bit more than I can stomach. For that reason, I am going to introduce a friend of mine, who will guide you through your journey. His name is Horris, and although he may look a little frightening at first glance, I think you'll be great friends when all is said and done. Unlike myself, Horris delights in the grim, the ghoulish, the scary, and the downright nasty. While I find it all slightly unsettling, I know he means well. He is simply... well, Horris.

You see, I think it is important to remember that Horris is not like you and me. Horris can do everything a character born from imagination can do. He will not be hurt if he loses a few fingers, or falls off a steep cliff. Horris can simply grow new fingers, or turn into a dozen black stones before he hits the ground. You and I have to be a bit more careful. So sit with him and listen to his stories, if you must. But I'm not sure I would advise following him into any dark parts of the forest. You really never can tell what he'll do next.

Good luck. I'm afraid you'll need it.

JRH
April 29, 2005

HORRIS' INTRODUCTION

Is he gone? Did he leave? Are we alone?

Okay, good! Here we go. Are you ready? I know you have more guts than Mr. Herrera. He's a scaredy-cat! But not you, right? Are you ready to read about twitchy, hairy spiders, each the size of a pizza pie? Are you excited to learn about what horrible creature might be hiding in your lunchbag? Are you sure you want to hear about Elizabeth of Bathory and the Bloody Fountain of Youth? Good! I have so many frightening things to tell you about.

What an exciting night we'll have! I'm so happy that I finally get to show someone all these secret treasures I have hidden down here in the basement. But wait: what's this? It looks like there is something moving around in that corner. I don't know what it is, but it sure is making some strange noises.

Should we look? I think we should.

Let's go!

HORRIS

THINGS
THAT
CREEP
AND
CRAWL

BIG, RED SPIDERS FOR LUNCH

SOMETIMES HUMANS EAT LOBSTERS. Have you seen this? I have. I find it especially fascinating to watch. They tie on a bib (like a baby), break open the lobster's shell with a little hammer, and hungrily slurp up the guts like they're delicious. Crunching, drooling, grinning, silly humans. Me, I just smile from the corner of the room and wonder if anyone knows that they are eating big, red, armored spiders. I giggle, but I don't tell them!

It's true! A lobster is in the same family as spiders, beetles, and centipedes! Just a big, red bug! What's more, these big ocean bugs have teeth in their stomachs! They use these teeth to help them eat their own shells, once they've cast them off. And don't let a bunch of them get near each other in a tight space. They'll turn into cannibals! This is why you see rubberbands around their claws in those restaurant tanks. And by the way, lobsters aren't red until you cook them. While they're alive, they come in all shades of green and black. Just like the bugs they are.

What strange oceanic insects, scuttling about in the dark waters with their large claws! What strange creatures humans are, eating them up like candy!

— THE NIGHT DWELLER NOBODY KNOWS —

THERE IS A CREATURE ON THIS PLANET so mysterious, that humans know very little about it. This sneaky critter burrows under the dirt, surrounded on all sides by darkness. It can hardly see, and has no ears, but it senses its prey in other ways. This midnight hunter sniffs to find his meals! Most importantly, this animal has a mouthful of pointy teeth it uses to kill its victims. Isn't that exciting? We call this subterranean hunter a "caecilian." (You'll sound like a snake hissing when you pronounce this: "Si-ssssseeeel-ee-un.") Chances are you will go your whole life and never even see one of these wriggling, tunneling creatures. Most humans have very small, weak eyes. Not like me. I burn holes in soggy clouds if I stare long enough. You, on the other hand, can't even see around the corner!

But I bet you have a good imagination. Think of a caecilian as a monstrously huge worm with a skeleton, or like a short, fat snake with a mouthful of long, prickly, teeth. The caecilian lives down in a maze of underground tunnels, and uses its dozens of needle-sharp teeth to grab small snakes, frogs, and lizards, and pull them down to their death! Ow!

Most people have no idea that caecilians exist at all, and wouldn't know it if one were right underneath their feet. Maybe there is one under you right now. Maybe it smells you from under the dirt! How would you even know?

MAN-HUNGRY DRAGONS

THE KOMODO DRAGONS are large, ferocious lizards—the largest lizards anywhere in the world. These tough-skinned reptiles grow up to ten feet long, and can run as fast as a dog! Imagine if you whistled for dear, old Fido, and a huge Komodo Dragon came galloping out of the woods! Wow. There's an exciting throught. Anyway, that won't happen. Komodos live on their very own islands, and I suppose that is good news for you. I don't have enough flesh on my bones to attract Komodo Dragons. (Although I did have quite a nasty little incident last summer, now that I think of it. It took me nearly an hour to get my head back on!)

You, on the other hand, would provide quite a tasty meal for a dragon. You'd probably even be a delicacy. For believe it or not, my small friend, high on the their list of tasty snacks are human beings. And why not? You are just another animal on this planet. And an animal without any claws, sharp teeth, or frightening roar! I'd say you are ripe for the pickin'.

Komodo dragons are so vicious, they eat their own babies. In fact, dear child, the young dragons have to spend their early years hiding up in trees to avoid being devoured by their parents. Imagine that! When the dragons get hungry, they hide in the jungle and wait for a goat, deer, buffalo, horse, or an unlucky human to trot by. Then, at just the right moment, they lunge out and gobble them up! Keep this in mind if you are ever on Rinca, Flores, or Komodo Island in Indonesia. And remember to tiptoe...

⊷ THE LARGEST TARANTULA ON EARTH ⊷

WOULD YOU BE SCARED OF A SPIDER as big as a pizza? What if this plate-sized arachnid lived underground and only crept out at night? Hmmm. What if it were strong enough to kill a bird? Does that sound scary to you? Will you think about this big, lumbering, hairy spider when you are falling asleep? Good! I bet you'll have very interesting dreams.

The Goliath Bird-eating Spider of South America measures about 12 inches across, is hairy, and hisses when upset! (But at least it doesn't shout like some humans I know.) This freaky, twitching spider hides in tunnels deep underground during the day and comes out at night to eat frogs, lizards, snakes, bats, pinky rats, and sometimes, even hatchling birds. Poor little birdies. But when a spider's hungry, a spider needs to eat! At least, that's what the spiders tell me.

See over there? Lurking in the moon's shadow? That's the Goliath spider, waiting. It stalks its prey in the dark; sneaking up, pouncing, and finally, injecting paralyzing venom with its giant fangs into the unlucky passerby. Another meal secure, the Goliath lumbers off to its hole, carrying its stiffening victim with it. Behind it, the Goliath leaves only moonlight, darkness, and a few stray leaves. Until it gets hungry again.

— THE WORLD'S MOST DANGEROUS SPIDER —

THE BANANA SPIDER is not a cute little pet. I learned the hard way. I tried to sit one up on my shoulder, and it bit me so many times I had to eat it alive. What would you have done? Anyway, the Banana Spider gets its name from the fact that it is sometimes found hiding amongst bananas that have been brought to the United States from South America. Its proper name is the Argiope spider, or the Brazilian Wandering Spider. You should just call it "Sir," though.

This spider has a nasty habit of hiding out in shoes or crumpled-up clothes, and nestling there until some unthinking human comes along to make things interesting.

The best way to avoid being taken on a quick trip to the graveyard is to shake out your clothes and shoes before you put them on! You just never know what's hiding in there.

This fun-loving spider has extremely poisonous venom, and enough of it to bite into you over and over again—which it loves to do. Mind you, unlike many spiders, the Brazilian Wandering Spider is not shy; it will not run away when it sees you. In fact, this creepy crawler has even been known to chase people!

So, open that lunch bag carefully, dear one! You just can't be sure what's going to come running out and chase you through the cafeteria.

THE TREES HAVE EYES

IN SOUTH AFRICA, THERE LIVES A SNAKE known as the Boomslang. The Boomslang slithers and lies about in the trees, and can grow up to six feet long. That's about the size of your father! Can you picture your dad slithering out of a tree with wide eyes and a forked tongue? I know I can! Would he still be wearing his tie do you think?

The bite of the Boomslang is very venomous and causes you to bleed inside, where you can't see it happening. But believe me, my dear, you can feel it. Without any medicine, a bite victim will die after a day or two of this bleeding.

And what a long and painful death it is. It's enough to give me nightmares! I still get twitchy when I think of the pain I suffered when I got stabbed by that beast's fangs. It's a good thing I can't run out of blood.

The Boomslang is known for its big, round eyes. What if one hid out on a boat from South Africa and slithered its way into your back yard? If there were one outside, you'd have to look very closely to tell. This tricky snake will change the color of its skin and eyes to match its surroundings. The Boomslang will stay still for hours at a time, waiting for its prey.

Have you seen any eyes up in the trees? Is there one hiding in the tree outside your bedroom window? Do you feel something staring at you?

THINGS THAT FEED ON YOU

OH NO, LISTEN CLOSE! I have a scary secret to tell you about walking around barefoot. I know it feels good. I love to rub my bare feet in brambles and glass and gravel, but remember, we are not the same. My feet are a lot tougher! For humans, going barefoot is not always such a good idea! There are certain tiny creatures that slither around in the dirt, just waiting for you. People call these creatures "whip-worms," "hookworms," and "ringworms." Sound ugly? Good! Now you're getting the picture.

These tiny, hungry creatures writhe and twist about in dirt that has been polluted with animal droppings, rot, and other disgusting, wonderful stuff. They just hang out, waiting for your bare foot to come along.

When that happens, they pierce through your soft and thin skin, and swim through your veins to your lungs and intestines, where they burrow into you and suck your blood! So wear flip-flops, or sandals, or wrap your feet in potato sacks, little human! Just never forget that to many of the world's critters, humans are but a tasty little snack. And the rest of us are usually very hungry.

HUNGRY FOR YOUR BLOOD

ALWAYS REMEMBER: There is more going on than you can see with your tiny eyes. An army of creatures we call "parasites" are living on your body! They are so small that they are invisible to you. But I can see them. And they are making a creepy, crawly carnival of you, even as we speak. Oh! Look at that!

Some of these parasites you actually need in order to stay healthy. In your mouth, you'll find the "tooth amoeba," who only comes out to eat up stray bits of food. These guys help you out, like elves coming out at night to do the dishes. Same with the microscopic dust mites on your forehead and your couch, who run around eating up your dead skin flakes. These are the good parasites. But others are bad, bad news. Hiding in trees, bushes, and maybe even in the cracks of your house is the tick, who really, really would love to climb or drop onto you, bury its head in your skin, and swell up from drinking your delicious blood. Not such a friend.

After a walk in the woods, check your neck, your ears, and between your toes! Run your fingers through your hair. Do you feel something attached to you? Is there anything crawling on you right now? No? Are you sure?

INVASION OF THE CANDIRU

HERE IS A TRAGIC TALE of warning. I speak now of my late friend Leevo. He recently met his end in South America, in the Amazon River. It was there he found out—too late—about the tiny and treacherous Candiru fish.

This dastardly fish hides out in the mud floor of the river until someone pees while they're in the water! Then, the Candiru

follows the stream of warm water until it finds the person's body, where it enters the same way the pee got out! This fish is an inch or two long, very skinny, and once it gets inside you it sticks its spines out, so it can't get out again. The candiru (or "carnero fish") then swells up from both drinking your blood and eating your flesh. This swelling makes the slippery, prickly intruder almost impossible to remove, and usually it ends up killing its host, and doing so in an excruciatingly painful way. I will spare your tender mind the gory details.

Let's just say that Leevo should've just held it.

A SHARK IS QUITE A TERRIFYING CREATURE to have after you. I can tell you that right now. I remember a certain night off the coast of Florida, racing a Great White to land as the streamlined killer rushed toward me. I should tell you now, no matter how fast you swim, you will never beat a shark to shore! You won't even come close. Even swimming as fast as I could, my leg ended up a chew toy for the shark. It didn't take long to grow back, but you wouldn't be so lucky.

If you were to cut your toe on a piece of glass or a coral reef, the mighty sniffing powers of this beast would detect that drop of blood—even if it were floating among a million drops of seawater! And if it couldn't smell you, it could sense your slightest movement. A hunter sniffing the psychic winds, a shark can even sense the electricity that your brain uses! A shark is a hunting and killing machine, plain and simple. That's why I love swimming with them.

I'll whisper something in your ear: While it's true that sharks kill about ten humans a year, it's all those human beings you might want to watch out for. Humans kill almost 1,000 sharks a year, collecting their skin for shoes and their fins for food. Yes, it's a dangerous world, child, full of senseless and unexpected death. If I had to choose, I think I'd rather be the human than the shark. To tell you the truth, I'm happy to say I'm neither.

A DEEP DRINK OF DEATH

THE LEECH IS YET ANOTHER SMALL, HUNGRY CREATURE waiting for some unsuspecting human being to come along and unwittingly provide them with a meal. The leech doesn't care about how this makes the human feel; it only cares about its thirst for blood.

Unlike you, a leech can drink and drink and drink and drink. You would get full and have to stop, but a leech can keep drinking until its entire body becomes bloated and black with blood. The leech is not limited by a sad little excuse for a stomach, tucked away in the middle of its body like yours. The leech grows to fit its meal.

Leeches are in the same family as earthworms, and can be found in shallow lakes and ponds. Back in 1799, Napoleon, a foolish little French general, had soldiers who learned the hard way that certain water is deadly to drink. I remember it well, as I was following along out of curiosity. These soldiers traveled a long way, and became so thirsty that they began drinking from any pool or pond they could find! Not very bright.

Napoleon's men ended up drinking a bunch of leeches that attached themselves to the insides of the soldiers' throats and grew so fat from sucking blood that the soldiers choked on the leeches and died! Hardly a worthwhile trade for quenching their thirst.

So, my dear children: If you don't want to die squirming and choking on fat, slimy little leeches, I recommend sticking to water fountains, and your sink at home!

PIRANHAS ARE MEAT-EATING FISH that are born so tiny, you can't even see them, at first. But once they begin to grow, they quickly become dangerous. Piranhas travel in groups (called "schools"), and when they attack in a feeding frenzy, the water boils and bubbles with blood and commotion. The sound is almost like a spooky sort of music.

Old sickly cows that bend their head low to drink from piranha-infested water have been grabbed around their mouth and face by the tiny fish with razor-sharp teeth, and dragged into the water to die. It's not a pretty sight, and believe it or not, animals can scream loud enough to give little humans like you nightmares for weeks.

It's not easy to watch a friend dragged down into the water, flailing about and bleeding from a billion bites, though. A school of piranha can strip the flesh from a person in minutes. All it takes is one dip in the wrong stream. Even fishermen who happen to bring piranhas into their boat have to be careful. A dying piranha could latch onto a toe and make it their very last meal! CHOMP! Yum. Old fisherman feet.

DO YOU SMELL SOMETHING?

YOUR BODY CAN BEGIN TO DIE, even when you are still alive. Isn't that scary? When this happens, it means you have "gangrene." Gangrene will make your skin turn black and your flesh rot. Gangrene will make you stink worse than a bucketful of dead birds. Gangrene will eat away your skin and bones until your whole body is dead. It does not make for a pretty sight or smell, and will most likely drive all your human friends away long before you drop. That is, unless you get the rotting part of you cut off by a doctor first. Or, if for some reason you are out in the wilderness where there are no doctors and you saw it off yourself (or gnaw it off with your own teeth).

Gangrene starts eating away at your body because of two things. The first is when the blood flowing inside your body gets stopped and cannot reach a certain area. When a part of your body cannot get blood, it cannot live. A bad case of frostbite, or falling asleep with rubber bands around your arm might do this to you. My body is filled with burnt sugar water, acid, tears, and cyanide. But you are much more fragile, young one. Blood is what keeps you alive, feeding your body nutrients and oxygen.

The second cause of gangrene is a very bad infection in a wound. If I were as tender a creature as you, I would be very careful not to leave any cut unwashed or open. Unless, of course, you think it might be fun to watch part of your body turn green, stink like roadkill and then drop off!

THINGS
THAT GO
CRUNCH
IN THE NIGHT

— UNDER COVER OF DARKNESS, THEY FEED —

THE COCKROACH IS A NASTY LITTLE BUG that has been on earth for about 280 million years, now—much longer than you and your kind. I remember them from the early, early days of Earth. And they are still better than nearly anything at spreading disease, and skittering and scuttling away from humans.

I love roaches! They vomit and pee on their food as they eat it. And they eat everything from fingernail clippings to old food on your dishes to their brother or sister or best friend. They are not picky, like you are with certain vegetables. Roaches are also very tough bugs with hard, crunchy shells. It takes me a whole lot of chewing before they stop squirming around in my mouth. And I have some pretty sharp teeth. Here's an amazing fact: If you cut off a roach's head, it will die after a month or so, but only of thirst—because it can't drink without a head! A cockroach has three brains in different parts of its body, and can even live if its heart stops beating. Not even nuclear fallout will finish off a roach.

Don't worry. They don't want to see you any more than you want to see them. During the day, they like to hide in dark crevices or in your favorite cereal box in the cupboard. But when darkness falls, they come out in little cockroach armies. So don't worry my child. It's only when you are sleeping that they begin crawling around. Sweet dreams!

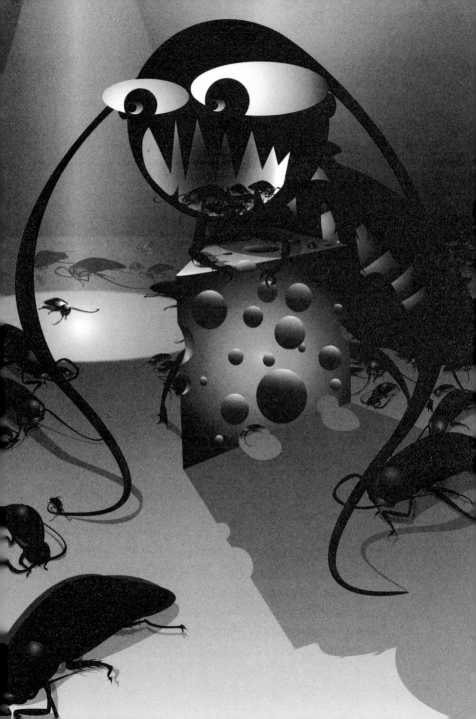

DOWN IN THE TWILIGHT ZONE

DEEP, DEEP DOWN IN THE DARK, DARK part of the ocean called "the twilight zone," a place where almost no light shines, there lives a fish with wickedly curving fangs and a habit of trickery. These fangs are so long that the scaly, slippery little creature can't even fit them in its own mouth! This animal, called the "viperfish," has a jaw that rotates open, and rows of sharp teeth that it uses to eat fish even bigger than its own body.

Some creatures that live in the very dark parts of the world and never see the sun have grown to make their own light. The viperfish is one of these. This clever critter has developed a natural light that grows from its own body, and hangs over its head. It blinks this light on and off to attract dinner (or breakfast, or lunch). Other fish see this light and swim closer, wondering what is shining so brightly in all the darkness. The viperfish will still not move. It will hang, motionless, waiting for these curious creatures to come just...a...bit...closer. And then, BOOM—the viperfish will swim as fast as it can toward its prey and stab those long fangs deep into the unlucky creature.

At least the viperfish's victim doesn't have to die in the dark.

THE BLOODY FOUNTAIN OF YOUTH

ONCE UPON A TIME IN HUNGARY, lived a Countess named Elizabeth of Bathory. She didn't want to age naturally, as all plants, animals, and humans do. She was so obsessed with her youth and her beauty that she had local girls kidnapped and brought to her under cover of night, for her evil purposes.

You see, the Countess believed that if she bathed in the blood of these young girls, she could stay young forever. Oh, if she would have only asked me! I would have told her there is no way for humans to stay young. And that's a good thing! Humans get wiser as they get older. Usually. Anyway, the murdering Countess was eventually caught, and she was sentenced to imprisonment until she died. Five years later, she did—walled up in a dark room in her stone castle. It was a gruesome end, although I must say, the evil woman got what she deserved.

You look so scared! Don't worry. Elizabeth Bathory is an old pile of bones by now. And you don't wander around alone at night. So you have nothing to fear, right?

BURIED ALIVE

HERE IS THE TALE of a little girl who met a terrible fate on Edisto Island, and was buried alive in her favorite pink dress.

The grown-ups didn't do it on purpose. They thought she had died. You know how grown-ups can be. Sometimes, they just don't pay attention. Also, this happened in 1850 or thereabouts—when there was a sickness called "diphtheria." (Trust me, diphtheria was a nasty little bug. It made my eyes bleed for days. If I were a soft little thing like you, I'd be dead for sure!)

So, this little girl woke up feeling quite ill one day. When the doctor examined her, he found she had come down with diphtheria. Soon after, the girl fell into a deep coma. The people taking care of her thought she had died, and so they immediately buried her in the dark, musty, family tomb!

Fifteen years later, when the girl's family opened the tomb to bury someone else, they found the little girl's bones, crumpled in a forlorn heap behind the big stone door of the tomb. She had died trying to escape. And that, my friends, is the unhappy ending to this little bedtime story.

THE MOST MURDEROUS FAMILY IN HISTORY

THERE ONCE WAS A MAN NAMED SAWNEY BEANE, who lived with his wife in a deep, dark cave on a cliff on the coast of Scotland. It was a dark, damp, stinking cave, and if you walked by it, you wouldn't see more than a few feet, for all disappeared into blackness very quickly. But if you could see into their lair, you would see human remains hanging on hooks, and bones stacked many feet high. For the Beane family—Sawney, his wife, their 14 children, and 32 grandchildren—humans were food.

That's right! The Beanes all shared the work, and divided the spoils. This creepy group of cannibals would hide out and ambush lone travelers on the dark forest roads that led from one city to another. They then killed the unfortunate strangers and dragged the bodies back to their cave. There, they would salt, pickle, and eat their human prey! The shady and sickening Beanes killed hundreds of people in the 25 years before they were caught (in 1435). When they were finally discovered, they were executed the next day, without a trial. The men's arms and legs were chopped off, so that they would bleed to death. The women were burned at the stake. Hurting people seems a strange way to punish people for hurting other people. But then again, I don't understand much of what you humans do.

So, if you happen to stumble across a deep, dark cave when you are out exploring in Scotland—or anywhere else—I suggest you stay well away!

➤ THE TWO FACES OF GILES DE RAIS ➤

ABOUT THE SAME TIME the cannibalistic Beane family was dragging victims back to their cave in Scotland, a man named Giles de Rais was doing horridly wicked things over in France. Giles de Rais was the original Bluebeard the Pirate, and I had the pleasure of stowing away on his ship once when I wanted a ride across the Caspian Sea. I'll tell you: The trickiest thing about him was how he seemed to be a good man, but hid many dark and evil secrets. Remember: Things are not always what they seem!

On one hand—and before he was caught—Giles was France's greatest hero. Oh, how they fawned over this dastardly criminal! Oh, how well he fooled all of them. He was a religious man, a lieutenant in the army, and he gave lots of money to sponsor religious music, books, and plays. That was his good side; his face for the daylight. His dark face was a horrible one, indeed. He practiced black magic, imprisoning and sacrificing hundreds of children, whom he lured to his castle with promises of treats.

Giles de Rais was eventually burned alive and hanged for his crimes. So listen well, my young and innocent friend: Never take candy from pirates you don't know!

PLACES WHERE
THE SHADOWS GROW

⏤ WHAT'S HIDING IN THE BASEMENT? ⏤

THERE IS SOMETHING DELICIOUSLY TERRIFYING about a basement, don't you think? In fact, many infamous murderers throughout history have used their basements to hide, imprison, torture, or bury their victims. Can you imagine having bodies in your basement? Even I can't see doing such a thing. But it's a gruesome business they conduct and I imagine they want to be in the dark while they work. The smell alone would make it very hard to enjoy my Rottenberry Pudding.

Sometimes I go down into the basement to rest. Once the bugs get used to me lying there, they begin to come out of their hiding places. Little crawly, creepy, multilegged insects scuttle about, slithering in and out of cracks and holes and climbing over my face. (It tickles!) My eyes quickly get used to the dim light, and reveal the cobwebs slung between mildewed boards. In my basement, there is a gaping hole in one stone wall, and no matter how wide I open my eyes I can't see into the darkness there. I guess this is no reason to imagine I see a wild-eyed crazy man staring at me from the darkness. Is it?

A HORROR IN AMITYVILLE

IF YOU WALK WITH ME, I will show you a house that may just scare the daylights out of you. It sits calmly in the pretty, peaceful town of Amityville, New York. It doesn't look at all like you might imagine a haunted house would. No boarded-up windows, no black, yawning mouth of a door, no devilish pig that speaks to children. Oh, wait. That last part isn't true. There actually was a devilish pig. Its name was Jodie, and it spoke to the youngest child in the family.

As soon as the Lutz family moved into the house that came to be known as the "Amityville Horror," they experienced some wonderfully creepy things. Doors unlocked and locked themselves; windows opened and closed themselves; all thumpalumping and knocking in the dead of the night. Scratching noises echoed throughout the house. Clouds of flies appeared suddenly, nasty smells came from nowhere, and green slime oozed from the wall—as if the house were bleeding some sticky, icky, alien blood. The Lutzes lasted 28 days before they moved out. I have always wondered why they waited so long. I was grinning from ear to ear, watching them scream and shiver. But I can't imagine they were having as much fun as I was.

So don't get scared if you hear a noise in the wall! It's probably just mice. But if a smiling, stinking pig wakes you up tonight, run! Run, run away!

THE CASE OF THE MOVING COFFINS

DO THE DEAD WALK? You ask me with a nervous voice. You want me to say, "No, no! Only in stories, not in real life!" Go ask Mommy if that is the answer you want to hear. Don't ask Horris, for I'll have to tell you the truth.

This true story involves a stone vault wherein a family of four was laid to rest. In the early 1800s, this was how many families buried their dead. Together, in a stone vault, with a sealed door that was not opened ever, except to bring a new family member in to be entombed.

Well, this spooky story that I now relate to you took place near a town called Bridgeport, in Barbados. Where nothing seemed to be unusual until the first time the workers opened up the family tomb to find the huge stone coffins within moved into a different arrangement than the workers had left them!

Well, strangely enough, it seems every time workers opened up the sealed door to bury another family member, they realized that these massive stone coffins had been moved around the room! They would put the 2,000-pound coffins back into place, and seal the door with cement. But the next time they opened the door, the coffins would be moved. Again!

Even putting sand on the floor to betray an intruder's footsteps showed nothing. It was a complete mystery to the whole town. Who moved the coffins? Nobody could ever figure it out, and I don't think most of them would like the answer. The things I could tell you about ghosts. They would turn your hair white. (Wouldn't that be fun?)

How did the story end, you ask? Well, finally, the governor of the town ordered the coffins to be moved to a new burial ground, and the haunted vault kept open forever. The town declared it an unsolved mystery, and it remains so to this day!

So the next time someone tells you there are no such things as ghosts, you tell them to come see me. I'll tell them the scary truth.

THE DEADLY DESERT

DESERTS ARE WHERE THE SCORPIONS TWITTER AND CREEP; deserts are where the snakes and spiders thrive. The day is a blinding, blistering time without a sliver of shadow, nor a tree in sight. There is only the sun and the sand, the sun's mirror. If you don't die of heat exhaustion or sun poisoning, you will probably only turn out to be a snake's victim, or a spider's prize. Or perhaps you'll freeze, once the sun goes down. The desert may be a blazing hot place when the sun is up, but when it goes down, the land quickly chills.

The desert nearly killed me when I was just a small thing. I thought it was nothing more than a big stretch of sand I might tiptoe across and be on my way. Halfway across the brutal land, I found myself dried out, stung, bitten, burned and dying of thirst. It's a cruel place, and I only suggest getting lost there if you enjoy frying like a little human egg in a big, gritty pan. And then freezing like an ice-pop at night.

The desert is really rather an amazing place...to visit. You wouldn't want to die there.

THEY'RE DYING TO GET OUT

THERE IS AN OLD ABANDONED GRAVEYARD in Chicago known as Bachelor's Grove Cemetery. You will find no road that leads you there, and you may have a hard time finding it at all with your weak human eyes. Yes, I think it's best if you just ask around. And if people show you the way, I bet they get a strange look in their eye first. They almost chased me out of the town! But I know my looks can take people by surprise. (And that's just the way I like it!)

I would talk you out of this trip altogether, but I'm afraid you simply wouldn't listen. So pay attention, because I will only warn you once. It's a scary place, with a long history of restless spirits. Keep away! Keep far away! There. I've done my best.

Anyway, once you make your way down the winding gravel trail that leads to the cemetery, you will see that most of the headstones have been either stolen or broken, and are now lost in the weeds and growth. If you are walking at night, you may even end up with an escort. For, since the 1960s, there have been many, many stories of ghosts, strange visions, and even a disappearing house. People say that on the trail there are red lights that move so quickly, they leave streaks in the air behind them. And from what I've seen, they move even faster than the humans making their hurried way out of the graveyard, terrified and running for their lives.

THE THINGS WE'VE DONE

LET ME TELL YOU ABOUT A PARTICULARLY BLOODY time in Salem, Massachusetts. It was 1692, right around Halloween, and a lot of people were feeling positively dreadful. The winter had been cold (for humans, that is), the town leaders were fighting, and all the townspeople were gnashing their teeth. Well, these people got together and made some bad, bad, terribly, scarily bad decisions. And many of their neighbors died some very nasty deaths because of these decisions.

In the Salem Witch Trials, it was almost as if everyone were sharing a fever of the mind. One girl got sick, and someone was reminded of a character in Cotton Mathers' book *Memorable Providences*. This book was very popular at the time. Well, the next thing you know, some people were being called witches, other people were swearing they'd seen women riding broomsticks, and the townspeople began coming forth, one after another, to condemn one another to death by hanging.

Later, almost everyone who had turned their neighbors in felt sorry and apologized. It seems a little time passed, and people began thinking clearly again. Although that didn't mean much to the 40 people who had died on the gallows.

OFF WITH HIS HEAD!

IN 1793, THINGS GOT VERY VIOLENT in France. You crazy humans! You were at it again. The government voted to declare a "Reign of Terror" against its own citizens, to make them obey the laws. Do you think this worked? Welcome to the French Revolution, a bloody time indeed. Luckily, I left just when things started getting out of hand. I barely escaped with my head.

More than 40,000 people were sent to their deaths by the government! They were not allowed to speak up for themselves, and once they were judged guilty, they were sent to the guillotine. The guillotine is a very simple machine that was designed to drop a metal blade down upon your neck so that your head is chopped off! Is that creepy, or what? Well, the guillotine became very popular during the French Revolution. The blade was almost 100 pounds, and you had to lay your neck down on a bench, facedown, to wait for the blade. When it fell, your head was sliced off, and flew into a big basket. The crowd was usually unhappy only because it was all over so fast. You should have heard them! Like a bunch of donkeys braying, or chickens fighting over scraps.

Humans! It's dangerous to try and make them happy!

I'VE BEEN WATCHING YOU HUMANS for a while, and all I can say is when you make up your mind about something, it sure can be hard to change it.

The Spanish Inquisition was one of these times. It was, more or less, a fight over which religion was the best one. One group of people felt their way of seeing things was the right way, and went about doing terribly cruel and nasty things to those who did not agree. Come back when you're a little older, and I'll tell you the rest. For now, let's just say that once upon a time, humans used very cruel machines on one another, trying to get one another to admit to things, or tell the truth. Or at least to get them to tell somebody else's idea of what was true. All of this may sound crazy to you, but that's how people were thinking at the time. As if skinning people alive, whipping them, hanging them on a rack, or leaving them in a dark dungeon with bugs and rats would get someone to tell the truth. But that's silly! Who doesn't love bugs and rats?

THROUGHOUT TIME, HUMANS HAVE DONE some things that might seem funny if they weren't so harmful. For example, let me ask you a question. What if an annoying little sparrow were singing at the window? Well, you'd probably leave the area, or cover up your ears, or shut the window. Maybe if you were feeling e s p e c i a l l y annoyed, you might yell at the bird, right? And if there were a movie that you thought was stupid, I imagine you wouldn't pay to see it. And if a writer wrote a book you didn't like? Well, I'm betting you simply wouldn't read it.

In the 1600s, however, there were a lot of people who thought it made more sense to burn all the books they didn't like before other people could read them! And not only did they burn all these books, sometimes they found the writer, and dragged him into the public square—in front of everyone—so he could see his books burning.

Finally, these (quite strange) humans would nail the writer's ear to a wooden post, so he or she couldn't move! This poor person would only be able to squirm and scream as he watched his work go up in flames. Is this what they mean when they talk about a "warm reception?"

THE GAME OF DEATH

SOMETIMES A CROWD OF PEOPLE GET TOGETHER and come up with some pretty frightening ideas. I have to give you all credit for that! For example, let me tell you about a fun-filled placed known as the Roman Coliseum.

Once upon a time (around 300 B.C.), in Rome, the capital of the Roman Empire, prisoners played games that ended in death. While everyone watched, they would fight one another in the middle of a huge stone stadium called the Coliseum. Not only would nobody break up the fight, but also there were guards who made sure the fighters couldn't run away. These fantastically gory fights usually didn't end until one person was dead. That's what the people wanted! This is your human race! The Romans would stand and cheer in the stands. They camped out all night long in front of the Coliseum to get a seat. These "games" were the emperor's gift to the people, and the people loved their bloody sport. They even helped decide if certain fighters lived or died by putting their thumbs up or thumbs down. So you see, those silly little hands of yours actually come in handy sometimes!

And this wasn't the only game! Sometimes live humans were fed to lions. Sometimes prisoners were lit on fire. Sometimes they were dropped from great heights onto the hard ground. What a bunch of fun-loving folks those Romans were! What a playful species you humans are!

STAYING FOR DINNER?

I WONDER WHAT A HUMAN TASTES LIKE. Well, it's not just those nasty Beanes in Scotland who know whether you taste like chicken or fish.

I know this because I've seen a few things, dear one. Humans eating humans is called "cannibalism," and it has been around for a long time, and in many places. Even now, on the island of New Guinea, there are still people who feel it's perfectly okay to boil, skin, fry, and sauté their friends and enemies. And they do!

Why did (and do) people eat
each other? Is it because they
ran out of fricasseed bats,
fried grasshoppers, or baked
cow tongue? Maybe. But usually, it has more to do with
what people believe than their
hunger pangs. Eating your enemies, to
some humans, was a way
of celebrating

your victory over their tribe. Eating your dead loved ones
was a way of showing respect! And then, sometimes people
have simply gotten lost in the woods without food and have
had to eat their dead comrades to survive! How tasty a field
trip that would be! I think I'm drooling all over myself just
thinking about it.

IMAGINE THIS...IF YOU DARE

DON'T LOSE YOUR HEAD

DO YOU REMEMBER EARLIER, when I was telling you about the guillotine? That's the machine that was made to chop off a person's head quickly and easily. Well, here's something I bet you didn't know: When your head gets chopped off in such a way, you still live for a while! Pretty nasty, I know. You actually have about 30 seconds before your brain dies. Thirty long seconds to wonder what that strange gurgling, dripping sound is.

But what happened in those 30 seconds to a person who'd had his head chopped off? Did he look over at his body and

THE FIRE INSIDE

ARE YOU WARM? FEELIN' A LITTLE WARM, a little hot, maybe? Maybe you should make sure you are standing near some water. Maybe you should be on the look-out for little black curlicues of smoke floating around

won-der who was lying there, bleeding from the neck? Did he reach his hand up to scratch his head, only to find a bloody stump? Did he watch his body reach its hands up to search for its missing head?

I wonder if in that short time without a head, you would try to sit up. Would you pick up your head and run away with it? Would you throw your head at the executioner? What would be the last thing you thought of, lying there, trying to speak but only sounding like wind whistling through a tiny hollow? I wonder.

83

THE MYSTERY INGREDIENT

OH, IF YOU ONLY KNEW MORE about some of the things you eat! I find it very amusing. Watching humans stuff their mouths full of so many strange things, like the big spiders I told you about before. And most of you have no idea what you are putting into your body, and don't even want think about it! It's all very entertaining. It's all very, fun to watch!

For instance, take fast food hamburgers—th yummy, greasy little treats. Do you wonder he made? Do you think hamburgers grow on tr think there is a hamburger tree somewhere Cows are made into hamburgers, silly. A take little pieces of meat, here and the cow guts, throw them away, and t entire cow—bones, poop, muscle, gr to head off to fast food land.

And that wiggly, sweet, gelat animal bones and skin! Oh lie to you. And bugs—I k dye that is used to co up beetles. Lip-sma when you sprin Mmmmmmm.

your head! Maybe you are about to burst into flames right this second!

Like poor ole Bentley, who was found in his bathroom burnt down to a pile of ashes. One of his legs was even still uncooked. Old man Bentley left behind a big smoking hole in the ceiling, and the delicious stink of charbroiled flesh. Nobody could explain how the paint on the wall wasn't burnt one bit! But I know. And I think you do, too—even if you don't want to admit it. It's a zany little dance called "Spontaneous Human Combustion," and it means that once in a while, people burst into flames all by themselves.

I know, you think I'm being clever! You probably think this is a ghost story, made up of nothing more than glue and gauze. But I have seen it with my own eyes. And it was not a pretty sight. Although it did warm up the room something toasty.

YOU, THE WALKING MEAL

MAYBE YOU'VE BEEN TO THE ZOO, and you've seen the signs telling you not to feed the lions. Or perhaps you've been camping and seen signs telling you to keep your food put away so you don't attract the bears. Why do you think they tell you this? Is it so the animals don't get fat? I bet that's what you think. Do you think the bear would be nice to pet and snuggle with, like a stuffed animal that you win at the fair? Do you imagine the tiger would purr and rub his head against your hand? Or do you think he would take a little sniff of your warm skin and suddenly open his mouth and tear off a nice chunk of you?

A tiger will eat about 50 pounds of meat a week, and it likes to rip it from the bone. How much do you weigh? Would you fill the bear up, or only provide a snack? Because that's what you are to tigers, lions, bears, sharks, wolves, and other meat-eating animals. You are a snack waiting to happen. And the only thing that keeps you out of their bellies are the metal bars on the cages. Without that cage, you are only a soft, slow-moving, funny-looking treat with a chewy center!

LOST IN SPACE

ONE OF THE THINGS I LOVE MOST about outer space is how very black the skies are. Blacker than a night on Earth could ever be, and stabbed full of sparkling holes. And I like watching humans, when they make their little journeys into space. I especially enjoy seeing them bundled up in their spacesuits, waddling around and tied to everything, so that they don't float away.

For example, when something needs to be repaired outside a spaceship, not only does the astronaut have to climb inside a big, bulky suit, but she also has to attach a tether to herself and all her tools, so that nothing floats away into space. Because there is no gravity in space, it would be very easy to float away, never to return.

What would that be like, do you think? Humans can't breathe in space. They can only breathe the oxygen inside their suit. But that wouldn't last forever. What would it be like to drift, alone and in silence, through the dark skies of space? How long would you live, before you were sucked into a flaming sun, or a black hole? And what would a scream sound like in your own ears, when no sound can travel in space?

➤➤➤ THE SECRET WORLD ➤➤➤

SOME HUMANS FEAR FALLING FROM A GREAT HEIGHT to shatter upon the ground in bits, but how many fear falling down into the Earth itself? For you do know, dear child, that this planet of yours is filled with hot goo, hard chunks, and unexpected pockets of air under the crust. Under the pathways and sidewalks humans waddle and shuffle across, underground fires burn in black caverns, near subterranean swamps, lakes, and crypts. What beautiful clouds of steam, smoke, and gas must fill the caves. How wondrous that there exists a whole world within this one!

Years ago, a gravedigger in Rothwell, England, fell through the floor of a church down into the Earth. He crashed into heaps of skulls and leg bones. That is how a secret crypt filled with the bones of more than 1500 humans was found beneath the Holy Trinity Church!

What other secrets are hidden under the ground? Well, in Centralia, Pennsylvania, USA, burns an underground fire that has been raging since 1961! Some clever humans burned trash in a coal mine and couldn't put the fire out. Today in Centralia, stinky, poisonous smoke leaks from the soil, blanches the trees white, and cooks the ground under your feet like a dirt-filled frying pan.

When I was just a small Horris, I would dig my claws into the dirt and imagine I could tunnel through to the other side of the planet. To tell you the truth, it still sounds fun. What a dark, scary, and fantastic journey that would be!

ABOUT THE AUTHOR

JOAQUIN RAMON HERRERA is a storyteller, poet, painter, musician, and photographer. He usually tells people that he lives in Brooklyn, New York. Joaquín studied art, photography, science, psychology, and finally, cinematography at NYU's film school, to earn first his Associates', and then, his Bachelor's Degree. Joaquín had fun in college, and still feels his most valuable education came from talking to the wind, walking in the sun, and studying his own heart, and the eyes and silences of others.

JOAQUIN SAYS THANKS: Thank you, Dear Reader. You have paid for my little book with money that could have been spent on anything. You felt what I made was worth it, and that means everything to me.

THANK YOU to the most beautiful of women, Carol Susan Ryan, for encouraging my art since the days I was drawing in milk puddles. Thank you for understanding when I came home from school in trouble for drawing instead of taking notes. Thank you for letting me mark up my bedroom walls until murals surrounded me in my teenage years. Thank you for never once censoring me. Hey ma, look: I'm still marking stuff up! (Except now they pay me to do it.)

SPECIAL THANKS to Hermoine Higginbottom (aka Christine Eva Bender) for doing the research for SCARY, and for helping in countless important ways. Thanks also to Sean Moore for believing in me, Gail Greiner, my fabulous editor, and all the kids at Hylas Publishing.

HORRIS is an Imaginary Friend, a gardener, and a very good friend to have on your side. He likes to look over the shoulders of children in trouble and make sure they are okay. Horris also likes to hang out with kids even when they are not in trouble. He has mighty powers, but knows how to use them carefully.

When Horris is not protecting children or planting Snake-Eyed Irises, he likes to fly through the morning sky in the form of a big, black bird and soak up the sunshine, or tumble through streams as a handful of black stones, to better learn the language of rivers.

Horris is a kind soul with a scary face, and the only people who get to be his friend are those who can overlook his frightening appearance, and he wouldn't have it any other way. Horris' favorite foods are deep-fried tofu sticks, black beans, and charred jalapeño peppers—except when he goes a little crazy over black jellybeans and Rottenberry pudding.

IF YOU LOVED READING ABOUT HORRIS and peeking into the world he comes from, then stick around—soon you can read all about his adventures in a fiction novel from Hylas Publishing® called HORRIS, LITTLE ELI, AND THE LENS OF TRUTH.

In HORRIS, LITTLE ELI, AND THE LENS OF TRUTH, you will finally learn how Horris came to earth in the first place, and witness some of the shapes he takes, and the magical powers he has. You will travel with Eli on his dangerous and important journey, and maybe you'll even make it back home.

It won't be a long wait, we promise! See you then!